MY FIRST BOOK OF THE
COSMOS

Button
BOOKS

SHEDDAD KAID–SALAH FERRÓN & EDUARD ALTARRIBA

Contents

Introduction

All galaxies, all black holes, all stars, all planets, asteroids, comets, rocks, dust, creatures, planets, people, atoms, particles, light... absolutely everything we know, and even more, is what we call the UNIVERSE or COSMOS.

In other words, the Universe is everything that exists: it is all space and time, and it is where all mass and energy is found.

Why isn't there simply nothing? WHY DOES THE UNIVERSE BOTHER TO EXIST?

We're going to take a trip through the life of the Cosmos from the time it was born until the time it might end, and try to unravel some of its mysteries.

GRAVITY is responsible for the structure of the Universe on a large scale, so first we will try to understand what it actually is.

WELCOME TO THIS AMAZING JOURNEY!

GRAVITY

You've already heard of gravity. It keeps your feet on the ground and means that when you fall over you bang into something.

Gravity is the force of mutual attraction between two bodies due to their mass.

If we put two bodies (for example, these astronauts) a certain distance apart in the middle of nowhere, they'll get closer to each other, going faster and faster until they collide.

GRAVITY IS ATTRACTIVE

In other words, it always attracts, it never repels. This means that "anti-gravity" does not exist. So there's no point in hoping that one day you'll have an anti-gravitational skateboard that floats in the air like in science fiction.

The more mass a body has, the more gravity it generates.

Two large bodies close to one another are much more attracted to each other than two small bodies far from one another.

The closer two bodies are, the greater the pull of gravity between them.

Gravity is the weakest of the four forces that govern the Universe.

The 4 FUNDAMENTAL FORCES OF THE UNIVERSE

1 GRAVITY is a force that is everywhere and is felt on objects that have mass. As we will see, planets, stars, black holes, and galaxies are formed thanks to gravity.

2 ELECTROMAGNETIC FORCE is responsible for electricity and magnetism.

3 WEAK NUCLEAR FORCE is observed in some radioactive decay.

4 STRONG NUCLEAR FORCE keeps protons and neutrons together in the nuclei of atoms.

Newton's Gravity

We all know that things fall to the ground, but Sir Isaac Newton (1643–1727) was the first to realize that gravity is a universal force: it is the force that attracts us towards the Earth and makes the Moon revolve around the Earth, and the planets revolve around the Sun.

The Law of Universal Gravitation

Newton came up with this law that described gravity as a force of attraction that acts instantaneously and at a distance between two objects with mass. It is as if two bodies were joined by an invisible rope pulling on and mutually attracting them.

The greater the mass of the bodies and the closer they are to one another, the greater the force that attracts them.

Why do bodies fall?

The Earth is a very big body with a lot of mass. All bodies that are close to it will feel its gravity and will inevitably be attracted to its surface.

If we drop an object from a certain height above the ground, gravity will pull it until it touches the surface. IT WILL HAVE FALLEN.

Why does the **apple** fall on the **Earth** and not the Earth on the apple?

An apple at the top of a tree also gravitationally attracts the Earth, but what happens is that the mass of our planet is so huge compared to the mass of the apple that it is barely noticeable.

Why does the Moon revolve around the Earth?

Imagine that you have a ball attached to a rope. If you start spinning around in circles, the ball will go around with you and as long as you don't let go of the rope, it won't shoot off.

Well, the same thing happens with the Moon and the Earth. Gravity keeps the Moon and the Earth together, stops the Moon from shooting off into space, and makes it revolve (orbit) around the Earth.

The same explanation works to understand why the planets revolve around the Sun.

(See p. 29, Why doesn't the Moon fall on the Earth?)

For Einstein, GRAVITY is not a force that acts instantaneously and at a distance, as Newton thought, but an effect of the distortion of the GEOMETRY of our Universe. Gravity is everywhere at all times.

Einstein believed that space and time were not independent things but were related to one another, forming what we call SPACE-TIME, which becomes distorted when there are bodies with MASS.

MASS "BENDS" SPACE-TIME

Let's imagine space-time as a kind of fabric that the Universe is made of, which becomes distorted in the presence of objects with mass.

Imagine that you have a flat surface made from a piece of fabric that can be distorted. If we throw a marble on the empty fabric, we'll see that it moves in a straight line.

But if we put a heavy body on the fabric, twisting it out of shape, we'll see that the marble follows the new shape of the fabric and moves in a curved line.

A SLICE OF THE UNIVERSE

Like the example with the marble, we can understand space-time as a fabric that the Cosmos is made of and that distorts in the presence of bodies with mass.

Einstein's General Theory of Relativity says that this distortion of space-time caused by the presence of mass is responsible for GRAVITY.

That's why we say that gravity is an effect of the distortion of the geometry of the Universe. An object appears to be acted upon by the force of gravity when it passes close to the distortion of space–time caused by a mass.

Although we represent the idea of the space-time fabric in two or three dimensions, in fact we should think of it as four dimensions: one dimension for time and three dimensions for space.

'FLATLAND'

In 1884, the writer and mathematician Edwin Abbott wrote a novel called *Flatland*, about an imaginary two-dimensional world inhabited by flat geometric shapes: lines, triangles, circles, squares, and others.

The main character, the humble Square, dreams of worlds with other dimensions: Pointland with no dimensions and Lineland with one dimension. The arrival of Sphere helps Square understand the three-dimensional world, but creates turmoil among the flat inhabitants of Flatland, who are incapable of visualizing a third dimension and understanding concepts like above and below. For them, Sphere is just a circle intersecting with the flat world.

We are like Square: even though we visualize our world in three dimensions, and know what above and below, in front and behind, and left and right are, we are capable of understanding that we live in a four-dimensional world: the three dimensions of space plus the dimension of time.

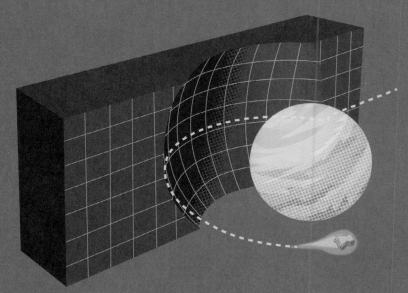

Like the example of the marble, a celestial body (such as a meteoroid) traveling across space-time can also experience a change in movement.

If there is no distortion, the meteoroid continues on a straight trajectory.

But if the space-time fabric is distorted by the presence of a body, its trajectory follows this distortion.

In fact, depending on its speed, it can enter orbit and even end up "falling" on the body.

Space-time tells matter how to move; matter tells space-time how to curve.

Due to its mass, the Sun distorts space-time. The Earth also folds the space-time fabric, but since it has less mass than the Sun, it causes less curvature than the Sun. So the Earth is more affected by the curvature caused by the Sun than the opposite. This is why the Earth orbits around the Sun. And the same thing happens with the Moon and the Earth.

SPACE-TIME IS THE PLACE WHERE REALITY HAPPENS IN OUR UNIVERSE.

Gravitational Lenses

As we already know, the shortest distance between two points is a straight line.

But what happens to light when space-time distorts due to the presence of an astronomical object?

Light travels in a "straight line" through space-time, but when it meets a massive object that deforms space-time, although light has NO mass, it still follows the curved space and so its trajectory bends.

We call this phenomenon a GRAVITATIONAL LENS.

If we were light, we wouldn't realize that we were traveling in a curved line, because all the physical space around us is distorting.

Thanks to gravitational lenses we can see very distant objects that otherwise we would not be able to see because their light is too weak and because a massive body, like a galaxy or a black hole, is blocking our view.

A gravitational lens works like a powerful telescope that magnifies and distorts light.

The first person who thought of gravitational lenses was Rudi W. Mandl, an amateur scientist who worked as a dishwasher in a New York restaurant. He explained his idea to Albert Einstein, who took him seriously and published a scientific article in 1936 explaining what a gravitational lens was and recognizing R.W. Mandl as the author.

Quantum gravity?

A GRAVITON is a particle that physicists believe is responsible for the force of gravity. Gravitons are similar to photons, or light particles, but so far no one has seen them. If one day somebody manages to detect them, it will be a huge scientific achievement since we will have found quantum gravity. Scientists have been looking for this for a long time.

11

HOW IT ALL BEGAN

The Universe is everything that exists, including space and time. But how did it all begin? For centuries, different cultures created myths to explain the origin of the Cosmos, and until nearly a century ago it was still thought that the Cosmos was static, immutable and eternal. These days, thanks to the observations of astronomers, we know that this is not the case, and that the Universe is changeable, dynamic, and expanding. Nowadays, the theory that explains the origin of the Universe, and is accepted by most scientists, is the **BIG BANG THEORY**.

According to the Big Bang theory, the entire Universe was a small, extremely hot and dense point.

Before that, this Universe was nowhere because nothing existed beyond it, not even space or time.

Around 13.8 billion years ago, this tiny singularity expanded violently, creating all energy, all matter, space and time. The Universe where we live was born.

Incredibly high temperatures

Opaque Universe

THE FIRST SECOND

From the first instant, the Universe began to expand and cool. At first, it was so hot that there was no difference between energy and matter, but as it expanded it created the forces of nature that we know *.

Suddenly the Universe inflated all at once and went from the size of an atom to the size of an apple almost instantly and, just after that, elementary particles that make up matter and antimatter (which has particles with properties opposite to those of normal matter) were formed. Before the first second of the Universe was over, it had grown by 62.1 million miles.

* Atomic, electromagnetic, strong nuclear, and weak nuclear

THE FIRST MINUTES

The drop in temperature enabled protons and neutrons to start combining into atomic nuclei. At the end of this period, the Universe was basically formed of hydrogen (75%) and helium (25%) nuclei.

380,000 YEARS AFTER THE BIG BANG

RECOMBINATION

The temperature fell to 6,332 degrees Fahrenheit and atomic nuclei were able to capture electrons to create stable hydrogen and helium atoms. Light was able to travel freely and the Cosmos became transparent.

Cold Universe

13.6 BILLION YEARS AGO

Clouds of hydrogen and helium gas came together and collapsed due to the force of gravity. If they were big enough and massive enough, they started shining because the energy from the fusion reactions of atoms inside them was released. The first stars were born.

As galaxies appeared, they formed galaxy clusters and superclusters.

The Universe continues to expand

13.2 BILLION YEARS AGO

THE COSMIC DAWN

The first galaxies were created: collections of stars, gas clouds, planets, and cosmic dust that stayed together thanks to gravity.

Right from the start, slightly more particles of matter than antimatter were produced and survived.

The Universe became a structure known as the Cosmic Web, a vast network of gas in which galactic clusters and superclusters were interconnected through dark matter, with huge empty spaces in the middle.

Many of the elements on today's periodic table, such as carbon, nitrogen, oxygen, and iron, were created inside the first stars.

GALAXIES

A **GALAXY** is a system of millions of stars, planets, cosmic dust, gas clouds, and dark matter brought together by gravity.

Galaxies can be different sizes, from dwarf galaxies, with around 10 million stars, to giant galaxies, with 100 trillion stars.

They can also be different shapes:

SPIRAL

ELLIPTICAL

LENTICULAR

IRREGULAR

Today, it is estimated that there are 2 trillion galaxies in the observable universe.

2,000,000,000,000 GALAXIES!

Now try to imagine how many stars must exist

When we look at the night sky, we can barely see a few thousand stars out of the millions that exist in our galaxy alone. It is impossible for our brains to grasp such a large number.

We are in the MILKY WAY, a spiral galaxy. Our Solar System is on the edge of one of its arms. It is so big that light takes 200,000 years to travel from one end of the galaxy to the other.

The galaxy next to ours is ANDROMEDA. It is very similar to the Milky Way, and is 2.5 million light-years away.

On dark nights, Andromeda can be seen with the naked eye but it is clearer with binoculars or a telescope. Remember that when you look at it, the light that you see left Andromeda not long after our ancestors had climbed down from trees and started to walk on two legs.

DIAGRAM OF THE MILKY WAY
(side view of the galaxy)

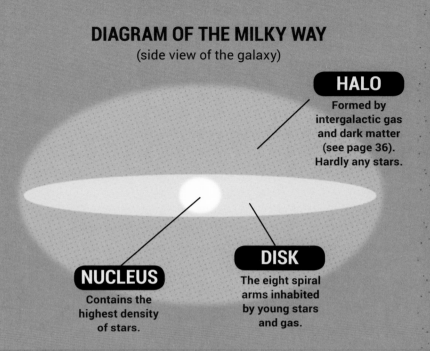

HALO
Formed by intergalactic gas and dark matter (see page 36). Hardly any stars.

NUCLEUS
Contains the highest density of stars.

DISK
The eight spiral arms inhabited by young stars and gas.

GROUPS, CLUSTERS AND SUPERCLUSTERS

Thanks to gravity, galaxies come together in groups, clusters, and superclusters that make up galactic aggregations.

Groups typically comprise a maximum of 50 galaxies. The group that contains our galaxy, the Milky Way, is called the Local Group and is thought to be formed of around 60 galaxies.

Clusters are much bigger collections of galaxies than groups, and can contain thousands of galaxies. The Virgo Cluster is the nearest cluster to us and is around 60 million light-years away. It is formed of at least 1,300 galaxies.

Superclusters are big groups of galactic clusters. They are one of the biggest structures in the Universe. The Virgo Supercluster or Local Supercluster is formed of around 100 galactic groups and clusters. It includes the Local Group, which contains our galaxy, with the Virgo Cluster dominating the central part.

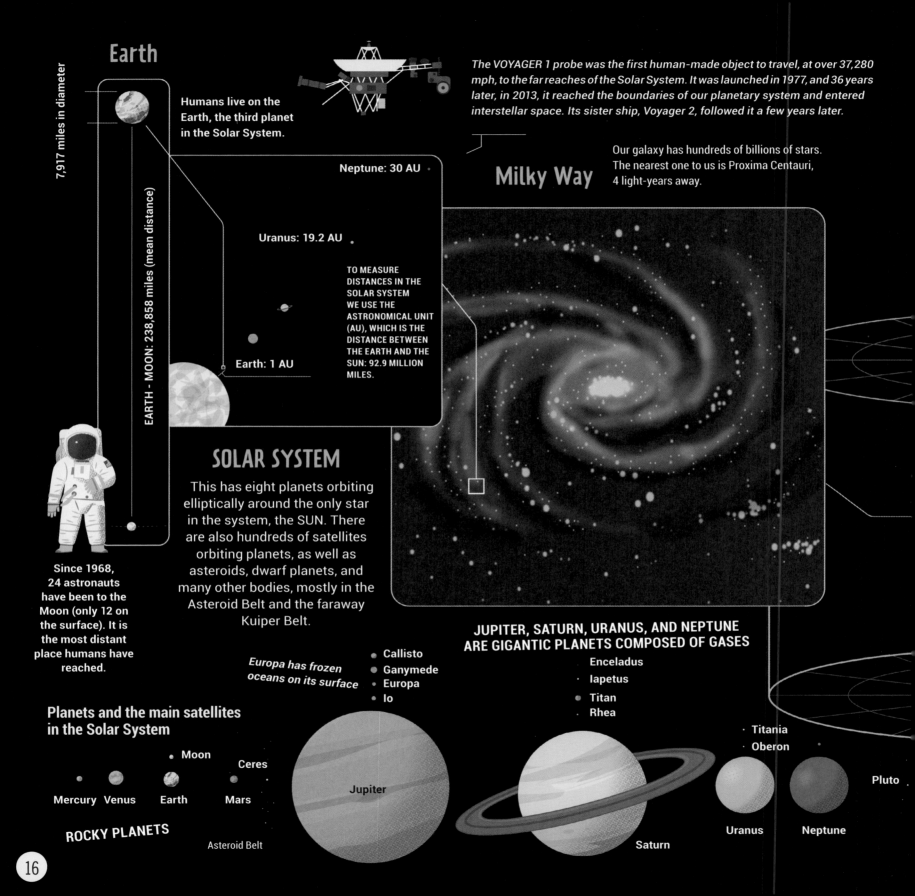

Earth

7,917 miles in diameter

Humans live on the Earth, the third planet in the Solar System.

EARTH - MOON: 238,858 miles (mean distance)

The VOYAGER 1 probe was the first human-made object to travel, at over 37,280 mph, to the far reaches of the Solar System. It was launched in 1977, and 36 years later, in 2013, it reached the boundaries of our planetary system and entered interstellar space. Its sister ship, Voyager 2, followed it a few years later.

Milky Way

Our galaxy has hundreds of billions of stars. The nearest one to us is Proxima Centauri, 4 light-years away.

Neptune: 30 AU

Uranus: 19.2 AU

TO MEASURE DISTANCES IN THE SOLAR SYSTEM WE USE THE ASTRONOMICAL UNIT (AU), WHICH IS THE DISTANCE BETWEEN THE EARTH AND THE SUN: 92.9 MILLION MILES.

Earth: 1 AU

SOLAR SYSTEM

This has eight planets orbiting elliptically around the only star in the system, the SUN. There are also hundreds of satellites orbiting planets, as well as asteroids, dwarf planets, and many other bodies, mostly in the Asteroid Belt and the faraway Kuiper Belt.

Since 1968, 24 astronauts have been to the Moon (only 12 on the surface). It is the most distant place humans have reached.

JUPITER, SATURN, URANUS, AND NEPTUNE ARE GIGANTIC PLANETS COMPOSED OF GASES

Europa has frozen oceans on its surface

- Callisto
- Ganymede
- Europa
- Io

- Enceladus
- Iapetus
- Titan
- Rhea

Planets and the main satellites in the Solar System

- Moon

Ceres

Mercury   Venus   Earth   Mars

Jupiter

· Titania
· Oberon

Pluto

Uranus   Neptune

ROCKY PLANETS

Asteroid Belt

Saturn

THE SIZE OF THE UNIVERSE

WE CAN ONLY SEE A TINY PART OF THE UNIVERSE, AND WE DON'T KNOW ITS TRUE SIZE, WHETHER IT IS FINITE OR INFINITE OR WHETHER OR NOT IT HAS ANY BOUNDARIES. IT PROBABLY DOESN'T MAKE MUCH SENSE TO ASK BECAUSE WE CANNOT KNOW WHAT IS BEYOND WHAT WE ARE ABLE TO SEE AND OBSERVE. HOWEVER, THE COSMOS IS MUCH BIGGER THAN WE CAN IMAGINE.

VIRGO SUPERCLUSTER

This supercluster contains around 100 galactic groups and clusters, and is dominated by the Virgo Cluster. It is around 33 megaparsecs across (1 parsec = 206265 AU = 3.2616 light-years) *110 million light-years*

THE LOCAL GROUP

This encompasses around 60 galaxies of different shapes and sizes.

VIRGO CLUSTER
(over 1,300 galaxies)

2.5 million light-years

ANDROMEDA

It is hard to imagine that the Virgo Supercluster is only one of millions of superclusters in the observable Universe.

Pluto and Eris are dwarf planets

Eris

KUIPER BELT

HOW IS A STAR BORN?

Like people, stars are born, grow, and die.

Due to gravity, the denser parts of the nebula start to attract gas and dust, and form clumps or fragments of matter inside the cloud.

Stars are formed from cold clouds of gas and dust in interstellar space called **NEBULAE.**

A protoplanetary disk is the material surrounding a young star. Planets can form inside the disks and give rise to new planetary systems similar to our Solar System.

Gas in a nebula is mostly hydrogen formed during the Big Bang. The dust is usually created by the remains of exploding stars after they die. As you can see, the Universe recycles stuff too.

Some of these clumps get bigger and bigger, attracting more and more matter. The cloud shrinks and becomes hotter.

In the biggest fragments of matter, gravity keeps compressing the mass of gas and dust.

It reaches a point where everything is so squished and so hot that the hydrogen atoms start colliding violently and fusing together, creating helium and giving off huge amounts of energy.

That is how a newborn star IGNITES.

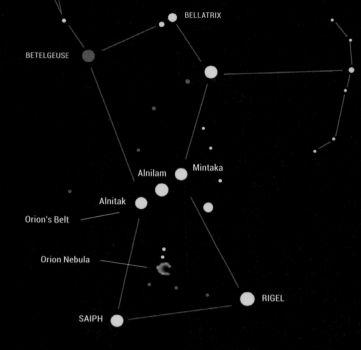

BELLATRIX

BETELGEUSE

Alnilam   Mintaka

Alnitak

Orion's Belt

Orion Nebula

RIGEL

SAIPH

ORION NEBULA

On clear nights, below Orion's Belt in the Orion constellation, a whitish patch is visible to the naked eye; this is M42 or the ORION NEBULA. It is a vast cloud of dust and gas where new stars form, and is like a nursery for stars.

If you look through a telescope, you'll see different young stars that have just been born. Astronomers have also found lots of protoplanetary disks.

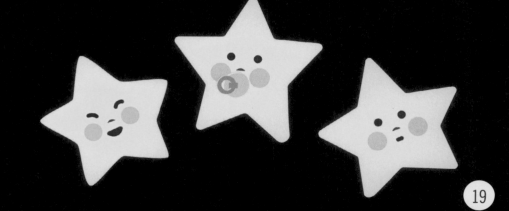

TYPES OF STARS

There are many types of stars: white dwarfs, brown dwarfs, yellow dwarfs, subgiants, red giants, blue giants, blue supergiants, neutron stars... and there are different ways of classifying stars. We're going to use the Hertzsprung-Russell diagram that classifies stars by temperature (color), luminosity (brightness), and size.

HOTTER — COOLER

<< 30,000 degrees Kelvin   3,000 degrees Kelvin >>

The color of a star is related to its surface temperature. Zero degrees Kelvin equals 523 degrees Fahrenheit.

LUMINOSITY is measured by comparing it to the luminosity of the Sun. If a star shines twice as much as the Sun, we say that it has a luminosity of 2 L☉.

COLOSSAL SIZES

It is not easy to represent different types of stars on a graph because of the huge differences in size. A red giant such as Betelgeuse, one of the stars in the Orion constellation, has a radius 887 times bigger than the Sun (but is only 19 times its mass).

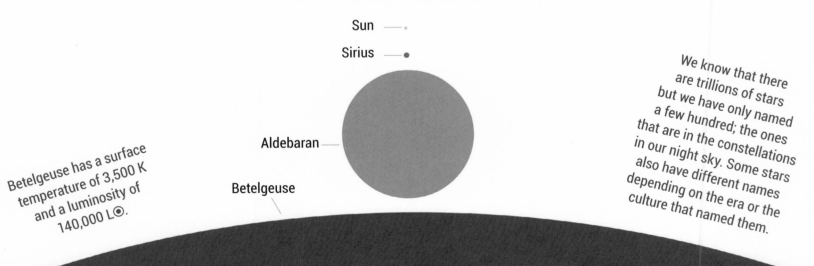

Sun

Sirius

Aldebaran

Betelgeuse

Betelgeuse has a surface temperature of 3,500 K and a luminosity of 140,000 L☉.

We know that there are trillions of stars but we have only named a few hundred; the ones that are in the constellations in our night sky. Some stars also have different names depending on the era or the culture that named them.

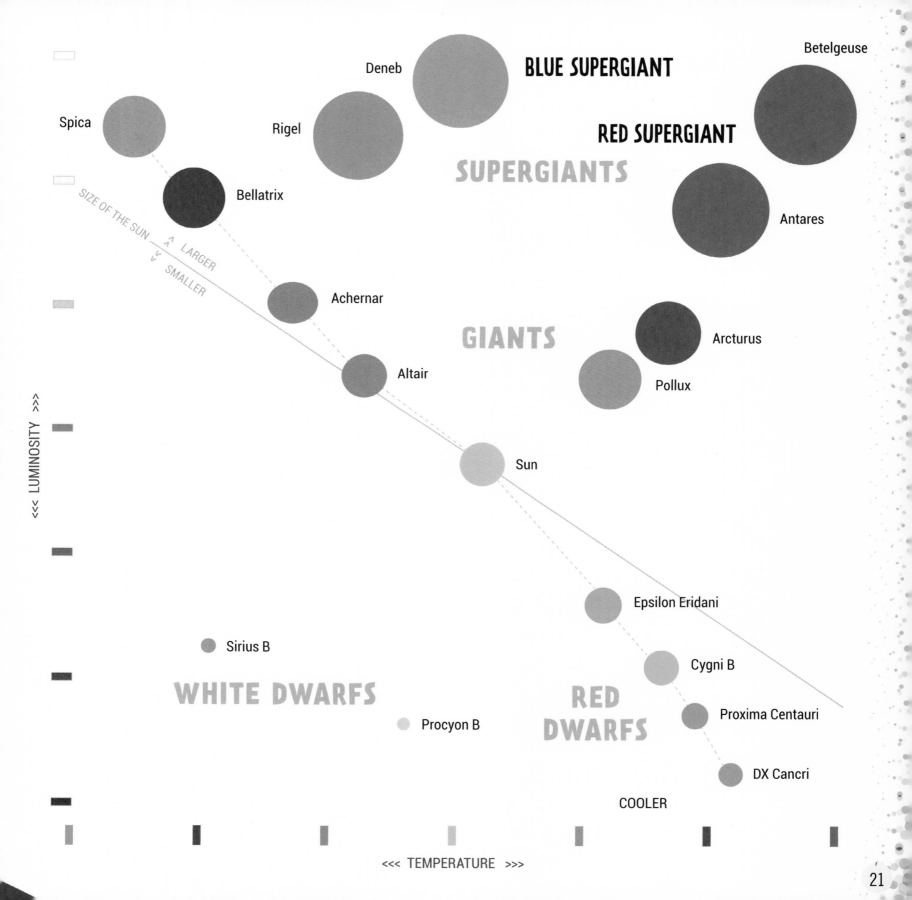

The life of a star

As we have seen, stars shine thanks to thermonuclear fusion reactions inside them.

NUCLEAR FUSION

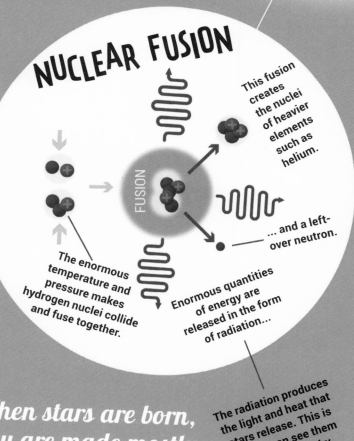

This fusion creates the nuclei of heavier elements such as helium.

... and a left-over neutron.

FUSION

The enormous temperature and pressure makes hydrogen nuclei collide and fuse together.

Enormous quantities of energy are released in the form of radiation...

The radiation produces the light and heat that stars release. This is why we can see them shining in the sky.

When stars are born, they are made mostly of hydrogen and this is their main fuel.

KEEPING THE BALANCE

FUSION

gravity

The huge amount of energy released by the fusion processes counteracts the pull of gravity and stops the star from collapsing. But when the star has used nearly all of its fuel, the balance starts to shift, and the star approaches its end. Not all stars are the same size when they are born. Stars that are greater in mass are hotter and brighter, but they also consume their fuel faster and their lives are shorter.

The Sun

This is the star that we orbit around that provides the energy we need for life on our planet. Like all stars, it had a beginning and it will have an end.

A star like the Sun takes around 100 million years to form, from when the first specks of dust and gas of the nebula where it is born begin to collapse under its own gravity until the heat and pressure cause hydrogen nuclei to fuse.

Stars the size of our Sun take about 10,000 million years to use up all their hydrogen while Betelgeuse, with a mass 19 times greater, only has enough hydrogen for 10 million years.

For now, the Sun has used approximately half of its hydrogen and is in the middle of its life, although it still has enough fuel left for about 4,500 million years more.

As the Sun gets older, it will get 1 percent brighter every 100 million years, and it will go through different phases until it turns into a red giant that will swallow Mercury and Venus. Earth will eventually become uninhabitable.

Finally, when it has used up all its fuel, the Sun will die and turn into a planetary nebula with a white dwarf star in the center. These glowing remains of the Sun will gradually be extinguished.

HOW DOES A STAR DIE?

GRAVITY   FUSION

As we have seen, most of a star's life is a battle between the pressure of gravity on its mass that tries to crush it, and the outward pressure of the energy from nuclear fusion that counteracts gravity.

But when the star has no more fuel to fuse, **gravity wins the battle and the star dies.**

But how does a star die?

It depends on its **mass**

LOW OR MEDIUM MASS STARS

(UP TO 8 TIMES THE MASS OF THE SUN)

These are the most common stars, more or less 97% of all stars that exist. They live the longest, and usually take billions of years to die. The SUN belongs to this group.

As they start running out of fuel, these stars get hotter and hotter inside but they also expand and get bigger.

HIGH MASS STARS

(8 TO 30 TIMES THE MASS OF THE SUN)

These types of stars have more mass, therefore more pressure and heat, so they do not live as long as the ones above.

When they have very little fuel left, they also expand and cool, but because they are very bright to start with, they go through phases: BLUE SUPERGIANT, YELLOW SUPERGIANT, up to RED SUPERGIANT.

VERY HIGH MASS STARS

(MORE THAN 30 TIMES THE MASS OF THE SUN)

Stars in this group have the biggest mass of all, and they go through the same phases as the high mass stars, only much faster.

Once they use up all their fuel, they expel their outer layers, forming a planetary nebula, leaving only a hot and inert nucleus, a **WHITE DWARF.**

The cloud of gas and dust starts diluting and can end up becoming part of another new star.

In this state, the nucleus of the star can form heavier elements such as carbon and oxygen.

This white dwarf gradually cools, and in around 10,000 years it will be completely cold, with no brightness, and turn into a black dwarf, somewhat like a rocky planet the size of Earth.

As their surface area increases, they cool and become red rather than yellow in color. They turn into RED GIANTS.

Red supergiants are the biggest stars in the Universe.

Heavy elements such as copper, gold, and silver are created in a supernova.

The supernova leaves behind an extremely dense nucleus, a **NEUTRON STAR,** one of the densest objects in the Universe.

To give you an idea of the density, a neutron star with a 6.2-mile radius has the same mass as the Sun, the radius of which is 432,288 miles.

HIGH MASS

FOR A FEW DAYS, A SUPERNOVA OUTSHINES ALL THE STARS IN THE GALAXY.

VERY HIGH MASS

The gravity is so huge that nothing can avoid being attracted to it, not even light.

When these types of stars are left with no fuel, the nucleus collapses due to the enormous gravitational pressure of their mass, and the star explodes. This then produces one of the most violent events in the Universe, a **SUPERNOVA.**

After the explosion, a large quantity of mass remains in a very small area, generating a huge gravitational field, and produces a **BLACK HOLE** instead of a neutron star.

We talk more about BLACK HOLES on page 30

IS THERE LIFE BEYOND EARTH?

There are trillions of stars and billions of planets, so it is highly likely that LIFE has emerged in other parts of the Cosmos, just like it has on Earth.

When we say life, we don't just mean intelligent beings capable of developing a highly evolved, technological civilization. Life has also evolved in many other ways like, for example, the different animals, plants, and microorganisms that live on our planet. There could also be other life forms that we cannot even imagine.

And although some form of extraterrestrial life might have developed a technological civilization, it could have died out millions of years ago and its planets might not even exist anymore. Or perhaps these civilizations are thousands or millions of light-years away, too distant for us to ever communicate with them.

Nowadays, scientists are concentrating on finding planets similar to Earth that have the necessary conditions to support life.

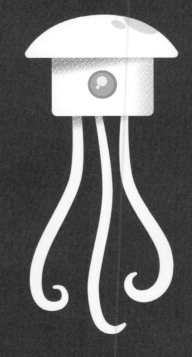

K2-18b

Scientists have found various exoplanets that could be habitable.

K2-18b is a planet that orbits the habitable zone of a red dwarf, in the Leo constellation, about 110 light-years from Earth. It was the first planet in the habitable zone found to have water in its atmosphere. It probably has a rocky surface and the right temperature to support life. This type of planet is known as a super-Earth, and is twice the diameter of Earth and eight times the mass, which would make it hard to walk on due to its high gravity. K2-18b is a much bigger world than ours but it is small enough to have continents and oceans on its surface.

The HABITABLE ZONE is the area around a star where temperatures are right for finding LIQUID WATER on the surface of a planet within that area.

Liquid water is essential for life on Earth, so astronomers believe an exoplanet in the habitable zone has a better chance of being able to support life.

If it is too close to its star, the surface will be too hot and there will be no liquid water. If it is too far away, all its surface water will be frozen.

EXOPLANETS

An exoplanet or extrasolar planet is a planet that orbits around a different star than the Sun. In the same way that the Earth and the other planets in our system orbit around the Sun, other stars also form their own planetary systems. Thousands of exoplanets of different shapes and sizes have been discovered, from large, gaseous ones such as Jupiter or Saturn to smaller, rocky ones such as Mars or Earth. Those in the so-called HABITABLE ZONE have the best chance of having the right conditions to support life as we know it.

Too cold

HABITABLE ZONE
Correct temperature

HABITABLE ZONE

Too hot

When we throw a stone upward, it rises at first but then gradually loses speed, before stopping and falling back down due to the pull of Earth's gravity. The harder we throw the stone, the higher it will go.

But can we throw the stone hard enough for it to escape Earth and reach space?

ESCAPE VELOCITY **is the speed a projectile needs to travel in order to beat gravity and break free of the Earth.**

IT HAS BEEN CALCULATED THAT THIS IS

6.9 mi/s (miles per second)
or **25,054 mph.**

As you can see, it has to travel very fast.

The escape velocity of a projectile does not depend on its mass (it doesn't matter how heavy it is) or the direction (we don't have to throw it upwards). It depends on the mass of the planet from which it is escaping.

The ESCAPE VELOCITY is not the same for all celestial bodies. Those with a bigger gravitational field will have a higher escape velocity than those with less gravity.

JUPITER   ○ MARS

For example, Jupiter's escape velocity is 37 mi/s while Mars's is 3 mi/s. The Moon, with a much lower mass than the Earth, has an escape velocity of 1.5 mi/s.

Why doesn't the Moon fall?

If gravity attracts bodies, why doesn't the Moon fall on the Earth?
Well, in fact it does and although it doesn't look like it, it is falling right now.

PARABOLA

If we fire a cannonball, it will shoot out in a straight line and, at the same time, start falling until it touches the ground. This is what we call a PARABOLIC TRAJECTORY.

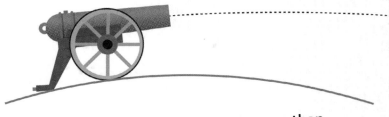

If we fire the same cannonball at more than 6.9 mi/s, it will be able to escape Earth's gravity and disappear into space.

CIRCULAR ORBIT

But if we fired our cannonball at the right speed (which would be very high but less than the escape velocity), it would be attracted by Earth's gravity, and slowly fall following a curved trajectory the same as the curvature of the Earth but it would NEVER touch the ground.

IN OTHER WORDS: IT WOULD ENTER ORBIT

This is exactly what happens to the Moon:
IT IS ALWAYS FALLING

Imagine an object with such
concentrated mass and such huge
gravity that its escape velocity was
more than 186,411 mi/s (the speed of
light). This would mean that nothing
could ever leave it, not even light.

Bodies like these exist in the Universe.
We call them BLACK HOLES.

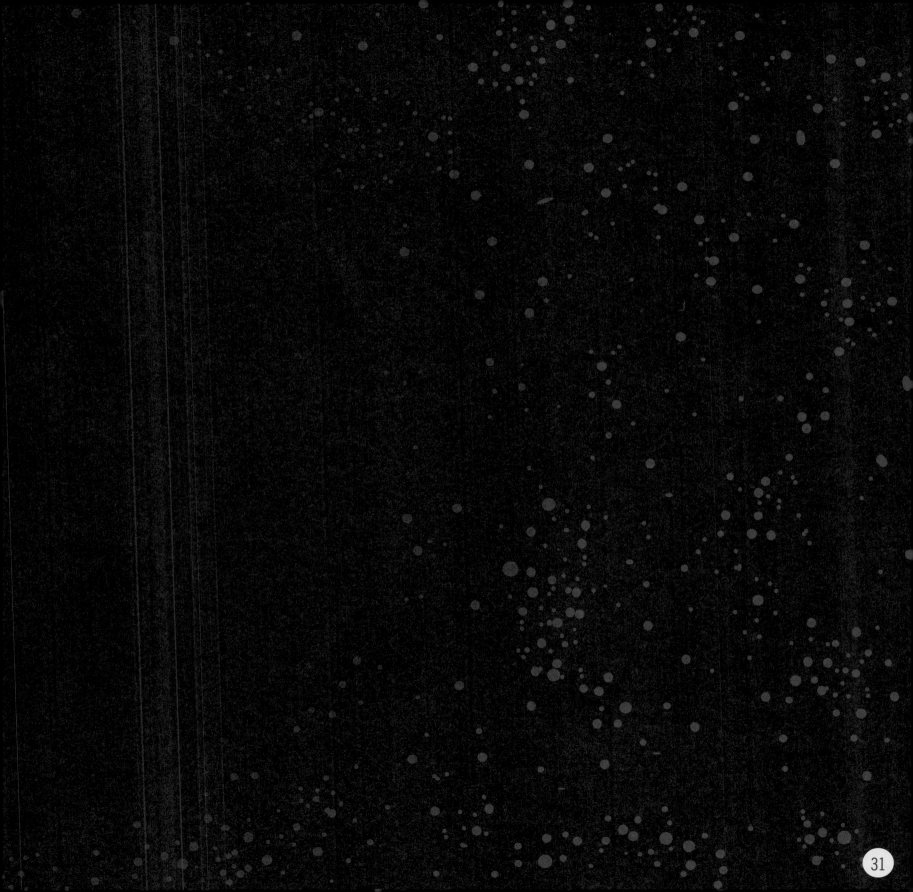

Black holes are singular objects in the Universe.

Huge amounts of mass are concentrated in a black hole and it generates such an intense gravitational force that it even has the power to trap light.

It is a hole in space-time that anything can fall into and nothing can escape. Its huge gravitational field is capable of attracting and swallowing anything around it; this dark giant can gobble up cosmic dust, comets, planets, stars, and even light itself.

WHAT'S INSIDE A BLACK HOLE?

We have no way of knowing.

BLACK HOLES
are BLACK because,
since light cannot even
escape from them, they are
dark and cannot be seen.

There is information inside, but we CANNOT access it.

The boundary of a black hole
is known as the **EVENT HORIZON**.

Anything that crosses this
boundary cannot come out again.

We have no way of knowing what is beyond
the event horizon. It is as if a kind of "cosmic
censorship" is hiding what's on the other side.

HOW A BLACK HOLE IS BORN

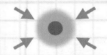

Black holes are born after a supermassive star dies in a supernova explosion.

If the star has sufficient mass, its gravity makes it implode and all its mass is concentrated in one point.

This violent event bends the surrounding space-time into a point, which generates a huge gravitational field: the one around a black hole.

There is thought to be a SUPERMASSIVE black hole at the center of most large galaxies.

What size are black holes?

Stellar mass black hole
They are around 10 times the mass of the Sun and very small in size, with a radius of only 18.6 miles.

Supermassive black hole
They are millions of times the mass of the Sun, and enormous in size with a radius equivalent to planetary orbits. These giants are thought to be found in the center of most large galaxies.

Black holes "evaporate"

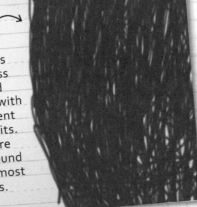

One of the strangest things about black holes was predicted by the great physicist **STEPHEN HAWKING**. He suggested that in time black holes evaporate and start losing mass in the form of radiation until they disappear in a huge explosion. This is what is known as **HAWKING RADIATION**. *although for this to happen, an astonishing number of years have to go by: 1,000,000,000,000,000,000... and so on, until you get to 67 zeros. (Age of the Universe: 13,800,000,000 years)*

How to detect them

We cannot directly see black holes but we can observe the effects that they produce due to the huge gravity that they generate. For example, they can act as gravitational lenses (see page 11), bending the light of a star behind them to make it visible. We can also see stars orbiting around something invisible. That is how we know that there is a black hole attracting them with its huge gravity, although we cannot see it.

What happens if you fall into a black hole?

Imagine that one day you trip and fall into a black hole. First of all, it's pretty unlucky. But what happens when you cross the event horizon?

It's no use calling to someone outside for help. They'll never be able to see or hear you, because no signals, not even from light, can escape a black hole.

So you fall in and as you approach the center, the pull of gravity is more intense on your feet than your head. It would be like two giants pulling you, and you would start stretching like a piece of spaghetti. You would end up being ripped into shreds.

COSMIC BACKGROUND RADIATION

Photo of cosmic background radiation, taken by the ESA Planck satellite.

This is the oldest image that we have of the Universe.

It is a map of cosmic background radiation (or cosmic microwave background), a type of electromagnetic radiation or "LIGHT" that flooded the entire Cosmos 380,000 years after the BIG BANG. **We're going to see what that means exactly.**

Photons are light particles. They have no mass but they do have energy and they travel in a straight line.

PROTON

ELECTRON

PHOTON

ATOM

A TRANSLUCENT UNIVERSE

The early Universe was formed by electrically charged particles, mainly photons and electrons. These particles moved very quickly, colliding with one another and making everything very hot. This is a state of matter that we call PLASMA, very similar to what is found in stars.

In this really hot Universe, photons continually collided with electrons and protons. With so many collisions, photons could not travel freely in straight lines. This is why the Universe was more translucent and opaque (luminous, but NOT transparent).

RECOMBINATION

As the Universe expanded, it also cooled. 380,000 years after the BIG BANG, it cooled down to 6,322 degrees Fahrenheit, enough for electrons and protons to combine and form neutral atoms. From then on, photons that had been wandering around everywhere were able to travel in straight lines. The Cosmos became transparent.

These first photons started traveling around the Cosmos and they reached us. They are the cosmic background radiation that we can detect everywhere in all directions.

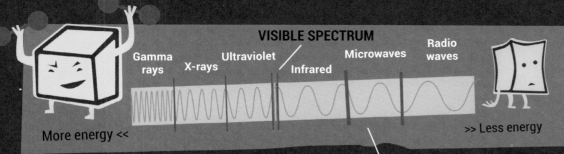

VISIBLE SPECTRUM

Gamma rays · X-rays · Ultraviolet · Infrared · Microwaves · Radio waves

More energy <<   >> Less energy

Light is electromagnetic waves but we can only see a small portion. We call this the visible spectrum.

The more energy light has, the shorter the wavelength.

As the Universe expanded, it cooled and these early photons gradually lost energy. Although at first they were very energetic and luminous, they now have very little energy left, and are in the microwave band.

The temperature of today's Universe is around 3 degrees above absolute zero (the coldest possible temperature). We know that because the cosmic background radiation that we detect is this temperature.

A JOURNEY INTO THE PAST

The Sun's light takes eight minutes to reach the Earth, so we see the Sun as it was eight minutes ago. Some of the stars that we see in the night sky emitted their light thousands of years ago, so we see them shining as they were back then.

The farther away we look, the longer light takes to reach us and the farther back we travel in time.

Cosmic background radiation is the oldest light that we can detect. Before Recombination, light could not travel freely, so however far back we look we can never see what the Cosmos was like before then.

Cosmic background radiation was first detected in 1964 by two American radio astronomers, Arno Penzias and Robert W. Wilson.

Their communications antenna captured an unknown microwave signal that appeared to be coming from everywhere. At first, they thought it was some pigeons nesting in the antenna, but after chasing them off, the noise continued.

Not far away, at Princeton University, another group of scientists was also researching background radiation. When they heard about Penzias' and Wilson's signal, they put two and two together and knew that they had finally found it.

THE MATTER THAT WE ARE MADE OF, WHICH WE CAN SEE AND TOUCH, IS ONLY A SMALL PART OF ALL THE MATTER THAT EXISTS IN THE UNIVERSE. WE DON'T KNOW WHAT THE REST IS. WE CALL IT DARK MATTER.

The Mystery of DARK MATTER

The ordinary matter that we know, called BARYONIC MATTER, is formed mainly of protons, neutrons, and electrons. In contrast, DARK MATTER barely interacts with anything, not even light. The only way we can detect it is through the gravity that it generates, so it needs to have mass.

What do we know about DARK MATTER?

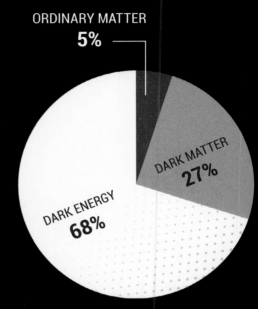

ORDINARY MATTER
5%

DARK MATTER
27%

DARK ENERGY
68%

👁 SEE PAGE 33

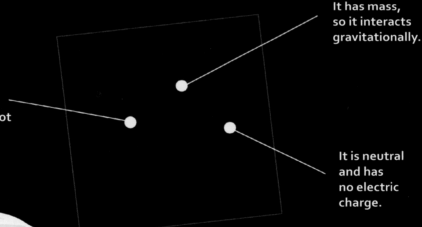

It has mass, so it interacts gravitationally.

It does not interact at all with light, in other words, it does not absorb or emit photons, so we cannot see it. In fact, we could say that it is TRANSPARENT matter rather than dark matter.

It is neutral and has no electric charge.

And that is all we know about dark matter...

In 1933, **Fritz Zwicky** (1898–1974) was the first person to suggest that dark matter might exist. Thanks to his observations, he realized that there must be invisible matter between the galaxies in the Coma Cluster.

Dark matter is abundant and comprises approximately 27% of all mass and energy in the Universe. To give you an idea of what that means, ordinary matter is just 5%. The remaining 68% is the even more mysterious dark energy (👁 see page 42).

Trying to spot dark matter
We know that dark matter is everywhere, but so far there has been no sign of it. Scientists are trying to track it down and there have already been a number of scientific experiments to try and detect the "particles" that form this strange matter.

It is thought that the particles that it is made of have very little mass, but it is so abundant in the Cosmos that its gravitational effects are noticeable.

How do we know that it is there?

Although we cannot see dark matter, we can detect the gravitational effects of its mass.

For example, if we calculate a galaxy's weight based on its stars (ordinary matter), then we compare this with its real weight deduced from its gravitational effects, we'll find that we're missing 80% of its mass that we cannot see.

gravitational lens

Another way to detect it is through the huge gravitational lenses (see page 11) that appear in galaxy clusters and can only be explained by lots of matter that we cannot see: dark matter, again.

Vera Rubin (1928–2016) was an American astronomer who found the clearest evidence of the existence of dark matter by studying how fast stars rotate in galaxies.

Stars that are farther away from the center of the galaxy should have a slower rotation speed. Rubin's observations showed that this was not the case. Instead, stars always rotated at the same speed no matter the distance from the center of the galaxy. This can only be explained if there is much more matter around the galaxy than that which we can see: dark matter.

Stars rotating at the same velocity in a galaxy

The cosmic web

The cosmic web is an astonishing large-scale structure in the Cosmos. It consists of gigantic gas filaments that connect galaxies and form what is also known as a cosmic spider's web.

It is thought that over half of the hydrogen created since the Big Bang is distributed in these filaments over 3 million light-years long that stretch across the intergalactic environment.

In the middle of the filaments, there is a large quantity of hollow or empty areas like bubbles, with hardly any visible matter in them.

At the points where the filaments cross, we find galactic aggregations, cosmic megastructures formed by thousands of galaxies that stay together mainly thanks to the pull of gravity of dark matter.

Galactic superclusters
are kept together by the
gravity of dark matter.

👁 SEE PAGE 33

The cosmic web
looks surprisingly
similar to the
neuronal networks
in our brain.

The Universe is expanding

George Lemaître

Alexander Friedmann

George Lemaître (1894–1966), a Belgian priest, mathematician and astronomer, and **Alexander Friedmann** (1888–1925), a Russian physicist, were the first to suggest that the Universe EXPANDS.

At the time, these ideas were not taken very seriously, but everything changed in 1929 when the astronomer **Edwin Hubble** (1889–1953) discovered that the UNIVERSE was actually EXPANDING.

Edwin Hubble

Hubble observed the galaxies around us, and realized that most were moving away from us and that, what's more, the more distant galaxies were moving away faster than the closer ones. Lemaître had also realized that, if the Cosmos was getting bigger, we could go back in time to find where this expansion began: the origin of the Universe, the BIG BANG! (Although he called it the Primeval Atom theory).

In the early 20th century, everyone, including Einstein, believed that the Universe was static and eternal: it had always existed, it had always been the same and it would carry on being the same indefinitely. After Hubble's discovery, the view was that the Cosmos was no longer static but was dynamic and changing.

We're going to see what it means when we say that the Universe EXPANDS.

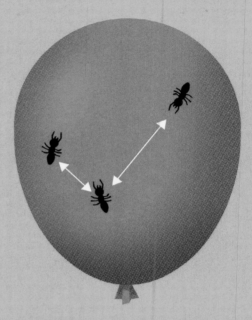

Imagine that we have a half-inflated balloon with a few ants on it, not moving.

If we start blowing up the balloon, we'll see that the ants get farther away from each other.

Each ant might think that it is special and is in the center of the balloon's surface, because, from its point of view, the other ants are getting farther away.

Seen from outside, none of the ants is special because there is no real center on the surface of the balloon.

Something similar happens with the Universe. As it expands, the space-time fabric stretches and everything it contains moves apart.

There is no special place that we can call the center of the Universe. Wherever you are in the Cosmos, you can see galaxies moving away from you, giving you the false impression that you are in the center.

It is space-time that is expanding!

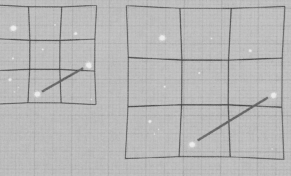

Since the Big Bang, the Universe has continually expanded, creating more and more space-time.

The Hubble–Lemaître Law

This law says that if we observe two galaxies where the farthest one (2) is twice as far away as the closest one (1), we will notice that, from our point of view, the farthest one is moving away twice as fast as the closest one. This is easier to understand with a graph:

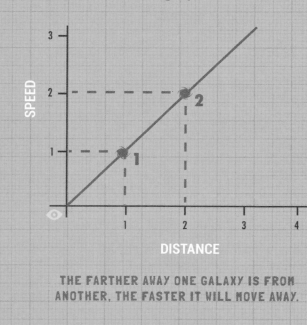

THE FARTHER AWAY ONE GALAXY IS FROM ANOTHER, THE FASTER IT WILL MOVE AWAY.

Dark Energy

Dark energy is a strange type of energy that fills the whole Universe. On the large scale, the predominant force in the Universe is gravity, which is an attractive force, but for some mysterious reason galaxies move away from one another.

You'd normally expect galaxies to attract one another because each has its own gravity.

For Einstein, this was a very odd idea. He imagined the Universe as a calm and static place, and he thought that there must be an unknown factor in the Cosmos that counteracted gravity. He called this factor the cosmological constant (Λ).

But as we have already seen, the Universe is expanding. The cause of this is the BIG BANG and DARK ENERGY is accelerating the speed of this expansion.

We don't know what DARK ENERGY is or where it originated, but we do know it is there, because it is the reason why the Universe is expanding FASTER AND FASTER.

Despite its name, DARK ENERGY has nothing to do with the clash between the forces of good and evil in the galaxies.

In 1998, scientists studying supernovas in distant galaxies discovered that those galaxies were moving away from us FASTER than they should be.

Back then, cosmologists knew that the Universe was expanding, but they thought that it was doing so in a uniform way, and that galaxies were moving away from each other at a constant pace.

When the scientists made this discovery, they were AMAZED to see that galaxies were moving away from each other faster and faster.

How come the expansion of the Universe is speeding up?

The answer to this puzzle is DARK ENERGY.

Although we do not know what it is, we think that it is responsible for creating negative pressure that generates gravitational repulsion on a cosmic scale.

Dark energy separates galaxies instead of bringing them together. And not just that, it moves them away faster and faster as time goes by.

Although we do not know what dark energy is, it is out there and, at the moment, it is the most important component of the Universe and will have an irreversible effect on its destiny.

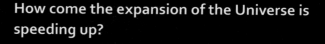

68% OF MATTER AND ENERGY IN THE UNIVERSE IS DARK ENERGY.

(So we haven't really got a clue what most of the Universe is made of.)

GRAVITATIONAL WAVES

Any disturbance in the space-time fabric caused by the movement of a body with mass generates a ripple in space that travels at the speed of light. This is what we call a **gravitational wave**.

CORK

WAVES

Imagine a cork floating on a pond. The water around it is still. If we suddenly fish the cork out, water fills the space where it was and causes concentric waves, or ripples.

The same would happen if, for example, we removed the Sun from its place. As we have seen, the Sun, like any other body, bends space-time around it due to its mass, generating gravity that attracts the Earth and other planets.

If we suddenly removed the Sun from its place, space-time would return to its original state, and the disturbance would create gravitational waves in the space-time fabric that would take around 8 minutes to reach Earth.

Compared with the other forces that exist in the Universe*, the force of gravity is very weak. Gravitational waves are difficult to detect because they travel a very long way to get here and lose energy along the way. They are so weak that although Albert Einstein deduced that they existed, he did not think that they would ever be detected! But technology has progressed so much that some gravitational waves from events that expend lots of energy can now be detected, like the gravitational waves generated after two black holes collide.

* Electromagnetic Force, Strong Nuclear Force, and Weak Nuclear Force

Waves in space-time

Two black holes colliding

DETECTING GRAVITATIONAL WAVES

On September 14, 2015, gravitational waves were detected for the first time.

They came from the disturbance in space-time caused by two black holes colliding 1,300 million light-years from Earth. This distant event was recorded by the LIGO Gravitational-Wave Observatory.

In fact, there are two LIGO observatories. Both are in the United States, and we need both to be sure that a gravitational wave has been detected.

VIRGO is the European gravitational wave observatory, near Pisa in Italy.

KAGRA is another gravitational wave detector, in Kamioka (Japan).

The LISA project

LISA is a highly sensitive gravitational wave detector that will consist of three spacecraft orbiting the Earth that form an equilateral triangle with sides 1.6 million miles long.

The distance between the spacecraft will be controlled by a high-precision laser. LISA will be able to locate and detect the tiny variation in distances between the spacecraft caused by the wrinkle in space-time when a gravitational wave passes by.

LISA is an ESA and NASA* project and, because it is incredibly sensitive, it will be able to detect waves that LIGO and VIRGO cannot.

*ESA: European Space Agency (Europe)
NASA: National Aeronautics and Space Administration (USA)*

The LIGO Observatory

The LIGO detector is a kind of instrument called an INTERFEROMETER.

1. The laser beam splits into two beams of light.

4. The reflected beams reach a detector that checks if they arrive at the same time or not.

The LIGO detector can pick up changes in the length of its arms smaller than the size of an atom.

2.5 miles

2. The beams travel through two 2.5 mile-long tubular arms, at a right angle to one another and with a vacuum inside.

2.5 miles

The two beams reach the detector at the same time (IN PHASE).

3. The laser light bounces off mirrors hanging at the ends of the arms

If there is the slightest variation in the distance between the arms, the beams reach the detector out of phase.

As the arms are the same length, the two light beams normally reach the detector simultaneously, but if a gravitational wave reaches the Earth, space is distorted and one of the arms becomes shorter than the other as the wave passes by, so the light does not reach the detectors at the same time. That is how we detect a gravitational wave.

1.6 million miles

Thanks to gravitational waves, astronomers will be able to study aspects of the Universe that have been inaccessible until now, such as the first instants after the BIG BANG.

45

WORMHOLES

As we have seen, space-time can distort due to the action of mass (or energy). It is like a flexible fabric that can collapse due to the presence of a body.

Imagine we have a sheet of paper and we draw two distant points on it. We want to join the two points with a pencil. But before we do that, we fold the paper in half.

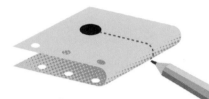

We can go from one place to another by following the line...

... or we can take a shortcut by punching a hole through the two points.

We can then get from one point to the other much faster by going through the hole.

If we wanted to go from one point in space-time to another, we could distort the space-time fabric to join the two distant points, creating a kind of tunnel to go through.

The two ends of the tunnel would connect two distant regions of space-time and we would have a way to go from one place to another extremely fast. We would have a

WORMHOLE.

A WORMHOLE IS LIKE A COSMIC HIGHWAY THAT CONNECTS TWO DISTANT POINTS VIA A SHORTCUT.

Imagine there was a wormhole between our Solar System and Stellar System Alpha Centauri, and that the entrance was in the living room of your house...

... and you could jump through it to get to your vacation home on the planet Proxima Centauri b, four light-years from Earth.

We don't know if wormholes exist or not. At the moment they are theoretical speculations based on Einstein's General Theory of Relativity. But it would be pretty cool if one day we could find or make them, wouldn't it?

Wormholes could also be used as TIME MACHINES. As they join points in space-time, we could put one between the present and the future. But how would we do it?

First, imagine that we find out how to bend the space-time fabric enough to create wormholes and put the entrances wherever we wanted.

Remember that they connect instantaneously. Even though the two ends of the tunnel are millions of light-years away, if you shone a flashlight in one end, the beam of light would instantaneously come out the other end.

ONE WAY OF TRAVELING TO THE FUTURE IS IN A SUPER HIGH-SPEED SPACESHIP.

For the friend who stays on Earth, the trip takes 8 1/2 years.

Spaceship going at nearly the speed of light

For the friend in the spaceship, the trip takes a few weeks.

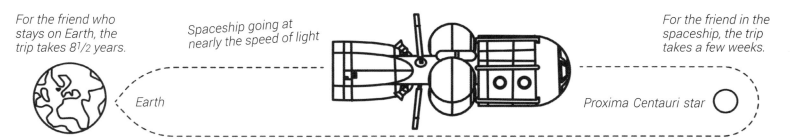

Earth

Proxima Centauri star

Imagine a spaceship on a return journey to Proxima Centauri, the closest star to Earth, 4.22 light-years away. If our spaceship travels at nearly the speed of light, the return journey, seen from Earth, will take about 8 1/2 years but, due to the dilation of time, only a few weeks will have passed inside the spaceship. This means that if two 12-year-old friends decide that one will travel to Proxima Centauri while the other stays on Earth, when the spaceship returns, the astronaut will still be 12 years old while the person who stayed on Earth will be 20 years old.

👁 **Less time passes for somebody traveling fast compared to somebody else who is at rest.**

GREAT. NOW IMAGINE THAT WE PUT A WORMHOLE ENTRANCE INSIDE THE SPACESHIP AND ANOTHER IN ONE OF THE FRIENDS' BEDROOMS.

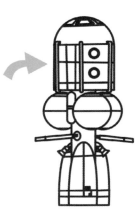

This means that when the spaceship comes back, the wormhole entrance in the bedroom is in the present, and the entrance on the spaceship is 8 1/2 years into the past.
We will have created a TIME MACHINE!

When you go through the spaceship entrance into your room, you travel 8 1/2 years into the **FUTURE**; but if you go through the room entrance into the spaceship, you go back 8 1/2 years into the **PAST**.

If it were possible to create wormholes, we could connect points in space-time by creating **TIME PORTALS** whenever we wanted, and travel many years into the future or the past. **INCREDIBLE**, isn't it?

WHAT SHAPE IS THE UNIVERSE?

Or to put it another way, what is its geometry? Is it shaped like a cube, a ball, a doughnut, a sheet, a baseball cap, or a spaceship?

How can we find out the shape of something that has us inside it?

If we draw a straight line on the ground, that's what we see—a straight line. If we make the line muuuuch longer and we go to space to look at it from far away, we'll see that it is not straight but curved, like the surface of the planet.

Although the Earth is a sphere, for a long time people thought that it was flat, for the simple reason that our planet is so big compared to us that we weren't capable of detecting its curvature. And if that's what happens with our planet, imagine what happens with the Cosmos. The observable universe is vast, bigger than you can imagine, and we can't step outside it and look to see what shape it is.

But what would happen if we drew some enormous lines crisscrossing the Universe?

The Cosmological Principle

The cosmological principle tells us that the Universe is isotropic and homogenous. This means that whatever direction you look in and wherever you are, you will always see the same thing. The Cosmos is more or less the same everywhere and there is no special place that we can call the center of the Universe. Thanks to this principle, we can rule out shapes that are not uniform such as cubes, pyramids, and baseball caps.

The parallel lines (meridians) that meet at the poles.

If we also include the mathematical equations from Einstein's General Theory of Relativity, the Universe can only be one of three geometrical shapes:

Spherical, like the Earth's surface. With this shape, the parallels end up merging and the angles of a triangle add up to more than 180°.

Hyperbolic, like a horse's back. The particular characteristic here is that the angles of a triangle add up to less than 180°.

Flat, which is the geometry that we are used to in our daily lives, where two parallel lines never meet and the angles of a triangle add up to exactly 180°.

ALTHOUGH THE MOST WIDESPREAD IDEA AMONG SCIENTISTS, MOSTLY THANKS TO OBSERVATIONS OF THE COSMIC BACKGROUND RADIATION (SEE PAGE 34), IS THAT THE UNIVERSE SEEMS TO BE FLAT, THE TRUTH IS THAT AT THE MOMENT WE DON'T HAVE A CLEAR IDEA OF WHAT SHAPE IT MIGHT BE.

The Cosmos is so incredibly huge that we can only observe a small slice of it. The visible part is what we call the OBSERVABLE UNIVERSE.

We don't know what lies beyond the COSMIC HORIZON. Galaxies are moving away from each other due to the expanding Universe, so we will never be able to see them. As the Universe expands, more galaxies move beyond our field of vision.

We can only see the light that reaches us, which might make us think that the radius of the observable Universe is 13.8 billion light-years; in other words, the age of the Cosmos *. But as the Universe has been expanding since the Big Bang, the light emitted since the beginning, has had to travel across an expanding Universe that is getting bigger and bigger. At the moment, the true distance between us and the horizon of the observable Universe is about 46.5 billion light-years in all directions.

46,500 billion light-years

* In fact, it is a bit less because, if you remember, the first light photons emitted were the cosmic microwave background photons during the Recombination, 380,000 years after the BIG BANG.

The Earth is not the center of the Universe, but it is the center of OUR observable Universe, a sphere with a diameter of around 93 billion light-years containing the objects that we can see.

>> TO INFINITY AND BEYOND >> We don't know what is behind the cosmic horizon, although it is probably similar to the observable Universe. Almost certainly there are galaxies, stars, planets, dark matter, black holes, etc., and they probably follow the same physical laws, although who knows?

WHAT IS THE FUTURE OF THE UNIVERSE?

It will continue expanding faster and faster, and the galaxies will move away from each other until they cannot be seen. After a very long time, the stars in our galaxy won't be visible from Earth.

Everything else will be dark and empty. The other galaxies will be so far away that their light will not reach us.

What's more, the Universe will continue cooling: all the black holes will evaporate, and all the stars will burn out as there will be no hydrogen left for fusion.

The Universe will become an inhospitable place that cannot support life anymore, so any living beings will have to move to another universe.

But that is all a long time away. Right now, it's best that we concentrate on taking better care of the planet that we call home.

THE COSMIC CALENDAR

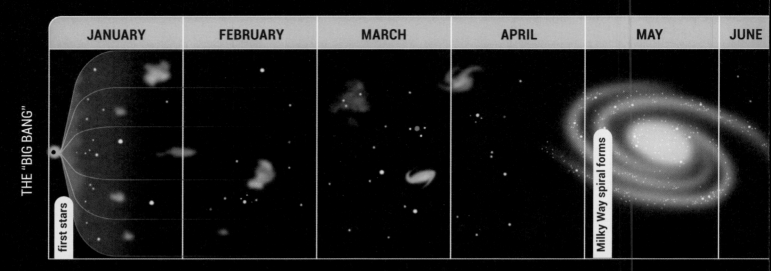

JANUARY	FEBRUARY	MARCH	APRIL	MAY	JUNE

THE "BIG BANG"

first stars

Milky Way spiral forms

If the current Universe is 13.8 billion years old, THE COSMIC CALENDAR compresses all this time into one Earth year, starting on January 1. Each cosmic month represents 1.15 billion years, a cosmic day is 37.7 million years, a cosmic hour is 1.57 million years, a cosmic minute is 26,238 years, and a cosmic second is 437 years.

The famous astronomer Carl Sagan made this calendar to help us understand the incredible timescale of the Universe in which we humans do not appear until December 31, and the whole of civilization is squeezed into the last minute.

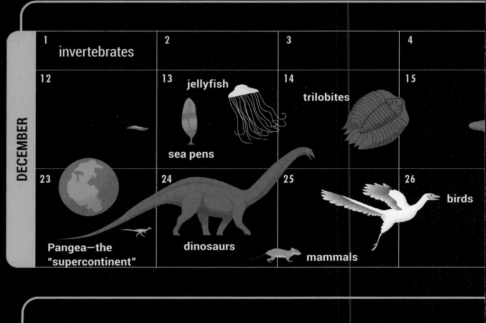

DECEMBER

1 invertebrates	2	3	4
12	13 jellyfish / sea pens	14 trilobites	15
23 Pangea—the "supercontinent"	24 dinosaurs	25 mammals	26 birds

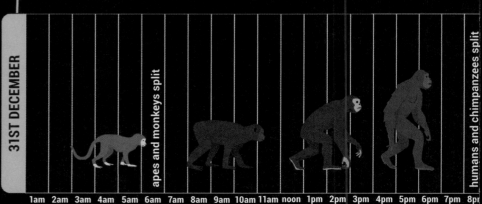

31ST DECEMBER

apes and monkeys split

humans and chimpanzees split

1am 2am 3am 4am 5am 6am 7am 8am 9am 10am 11am noon 1pm 2pm 3pm 4pm 5pm 6pm 7pm 8pm

54